Hinemoa And Tutanekai: A Maori Legend With Other Stories And Some Verses - Primary Source Edition

Rathmell Wilson

"HINEMOA," "A Child's Soul," and "Venus and Tannhäuser" first appeared in "The Shirburnian" (Sherborne School Magazine).

"The Last Grim Joke," "Concerning a Literary Gentleman and a Spirit," "The Want," and "A Might-have-been" were first published in "The 'Varsity" (Oxford).

"The Tale of a Ladies' Man," the verses "A Fairy's Bower" introduced into the story of "The Singing Girl," "A Girl and a Poet," number one of the "Verses to a Dead Girl," "A Silver Ring," "Evasion," and "At a Dance" appeared in "The Dorset and Somerset Standard," when I wrote "Tittle-Tattle" weekly in its columns.

"The Athlete and the Aesthete" appeared in "The Mermaid" (Birmingham University Magazine).

I render thanks to the editors of these papers for permission to reprint.

The additions in this new edition are an Author's Note, paragraphs in "The Singing Girl," "A Girl and a Poet," "The Hippo' Maniac" and "A Might-have-been," "A Challenge Accepted," "The Silver Lining," also a few quotations,—and the whole book has been revised.

R. W.

AUTHOR'S NOTE TO THE NEW EDITION

A SPRING book written most of it in the spring-time of the year, and all of it in the springtime of my life.

Thus would I describe this small collection of writings.

When I read it I always find myself thinking of Oxford by moonlight—one of the most beautiful scenes imaginable—So much of this book was thought of at Oxford by moonlight !

And many ideas for it came to me in the dim cloisters of an old-world school in Dorsetshire, and some in Paris, which seems with Oxford to share the spirit of everlasting youth.

(I have heard Oxford described as "Alma Mater, old yet ever young," but to my mind this is too horribly suggestive of an enamelled dowager !)

I also am indebted for many thoughts to the

garden of St. John the Divine, which has inherited much of its patron's divinity !   And to many other charming places—and people !

The spring writer of verses is ever one who strives—however unsuccessfully—after beauty.

And in that striving is to be found great joy— especially if he be spared the agony of "pot-boiling " !

Many will scoff, but always there will be the charming few who will understand.

He will soon become acquainted with the literary rhinoceros.

No one in the least sense of the word an artist can ever wish for " praise, praise, praise."

If criticism is " the art of praise " it is a lost art, but it certainly is not the art of abuse !

He cannot fail to despise unqualified rudeness, (often misnamed epigram) as much as he despises fulsome flattery.

Surely the noblest function of criticism is to help artists to come nearer their ideals—a small book is often worthy of much notice.

This is exactly what the literary rhinoceros never does. He revels in abuse without reason, but refuses to give reason without abuse!

Those who understand recognise in all such spring books as this big ideals in small achievements.

These are the people I wish to thank, and especially the professional critics among them.

It is because they have understood so well that I am able to add these few words to a new edition!

RATHMELL WILSON.

27th of October, 1906.

CONTENTS

TO ESMÊ

THE MAORI LEGEND OF HINEMOA AND TUTANEKAI

TOLD IN PROSE AND LYRICS

A Foreword

Listen to a Maori legend,
  To a tale of love and war,
Hear how love o'er battle triumphed,
  As so many times before !

I will tell it in the evening,
  When the stars begin to shine,
When our thoughts are very solemn,
  Full of fancies half-divine.

Hear a tale of strange adventure,
  Which to wonderment may move,
How a warrior found his lady,
  How the lady learned to love.

I will tell it when the shadows
   Hover in a mystic light,
When the tall sad trees are whispering
   Wondrous secrets to the night.

Listen to a Maori legend,
   To a tale of love and war,
Hear how light shone through the darkness,
   As so many times before !

THE tribe of the Princess Hinemoa was at war with that of a great chief.

Fierce was the conflict, and for many sad weeks the land was the scene of cruel battles, and every moment anxious hearts dreaded some terrible news of slaughter or fresh danger.

The Princess was beautiful as some tall, stately palm-tree, and pure as any of the summer flowers.

Although she hated her adversary with a bitter hatred, yet she dearly loved Tutanekai, his younger son.

He lived on the island of Mokoia in the Roturua Lake, on the shore of which she had her own small hut wherein she often dwelt in times of peace.

Tutanekai loved her with a great love. All his thoughts were of her, and he dreamed of her at night, so that in the midst of war and sorrow, love was reigning in these two hearts, and the affairs of State seemed very, very trivial when compared with the affairs of Love!

Every evening Tutanekai used to sit with Tiki, his great friend, on the shore of the island, when the stars began to shine and the moon shed a silver glow upon the water; and, even in time of war, they played upon the lute and horn.

Sometimes they played bright airs, but very often Tutanekai would play alone—sad, wistful music,—as he gazed across the lake towards the place where he fancied Hinemoa would be—or would sing quaint songs.

He was always wondering, "Does she love me? Does she love me?"

He little knew then that every evening, at great risk, she stole down to her small hut and waited for his playing, which was to her the sweetest thing on earth.

But at last he could restrain himself no longer, and, at his request, Tiki went across the water and gave Hinemoa

TUTANEKAI'S LOVE-SONG

"Hinemoa! Hinemoa!
   Night and day I long for thee,
Hinemoa! Hinemoa!
   Come to me, oh! come to me!

" Once I dreamed a dream by moonlight,
 Saw thee seated at my side,
Took thy little hands and kissed them,
 Brought thee home to be my bride.

" Then the vision sadly faded,
 And I was alone again,
Yet the fairies gently whispered,
 That I should not plead in vain.

" Hinemoa ! Hinemoa !
 Thou wast born my bride to be.
Hinemoa ! Hinemoa !
 Come to me, oh ! come to me ! "

When Hinemoa received this love-song her heart beat with ecstasy.

The world seemed lovelier, the birds more cheerful, the flowers fairer, the grass greener than ever before.

Tiki watched her, and, for his friend's sake, he was very happy.

He could well see that the whispered prophecy of the fairies would be fulfilled.

Hinemoa smiled on him—a radiant smile. Then she became rather shy, but she gave him a little song, and begged of him to take it back to her lover with " all her heart."   This was

Hinemoa's Reply

" I will speed across the lake,
　Risking all for thy dear sake.
　Now I know thy love is sure,
　Love shall triumph over war.
　　I am thine ;
　And thou, oh, joy ! art mine.

" I have loved thee very long :
　When I heard thy distant song,
　Every evening I would listen,
　Till my eyes with tears would glisten,
　　For I sighed
　To be, for aye, thy bride.

" As I journey 'neath the moon,
　Play some pretty festal tune,
　Which shall save me from alarms,
　Which shall guide me to thy arms,
　　There to be,
　For ever, dear, with thee ! "

Then, when they at last both knew that they were
really to belong to one another, each began to wonder

what strange power had drawn them together, and how they had first discovered that they were meant to be lovers, and each decided that one can only say, "The ways of love are strange," as so many have decided since, and will decide until the end of time!

The evening on which Hinemoa was to escape to the island was very dark, and her heart was full of mingled fear and happiness.

In the far distance she could hear the lute-calls of Tutanekai with Tiki's horn, and the music brought her much comfort and strength.

Then suddenly all joy left her, she groaned in sorrow and fell weeping on the shore.

For her people, in some way suspecting her heart's secret, had taken away the canoe in which she was to escape.

As she lay sobbing, her long, dark hair falling over her shoulders, the music from the island sounded more distinctly.

It was merry music, for Tutanekai was no longer sad and doubtful, but very happy, and the lute uttered the joyful expectation in his soul.

But for Hinemoa all was darkness and agony. It seemed as if the moon and stars had vanished from her life, and the playing seemed like death-music for her happiness.

Then the air was filled with fairy voices—very soft, like gentle breezes. Hinemoa in her sorrow listened, and this is

WHAT THE FAIRIES SANG

" Lovely lady, do not fear,
 We thy sorrows now may cheer,
 Though thy people plot against thee,
 Fairies will not plot against thee,
 Plunge into the lake and swim.

" Listen to thy lover's song,
 Though the way is sadly long,
 O'er the water we will guide thee,
 Very gently we will guide thee,
 Till we bring thee safe to him."

Slowly the song died away.

Then Hinemoa, taking heart, flung her frail form into the silent lake.

It was a long, long journey, and many times she almost lost all hope, and determined to let herself sink beneath the water ; but the fairies always held her up, and at last brought her to the shore of Mokoia. Then they left her, singing as they sped away.

The music of the lute and horn now sounded very near, but Hinemoa could only throw herself down by a pool and, from utter weariness, fall asleep.

The music was her lullaby, and she dreamed happy dreams of Tutanekai, never thinking of the anxious sorrow she would cause him. He played until late into the night, yet Hinemoa never came. He never doubted her love, only feared some evil had come to her; but at last he ceased his playing, and seemed half mad with terror.

Tiki could not comfort him, and feared for his mind, so wild were his ravings. He rushed to and fro on the shore, crying, "Hinemoa! Hinemoa! Hinemoa!" but the only answer was a mocking echo.

At last he came to the side of the pool and found her.

She was sleeping peacefully, smiling as she dreamed of him, looking tired but very pretty.

With a cry of joy he clasped her in his arms. He soon understood all.

So let us leave them, full of happiness, beginning that life of love which they desire more than aught else, while the morning light and the sun rising upon the lake are emblems of a dawning peace.

AN AFTERWORD

It is told—the Maori legend,
  Love has triumphed over war,
Now the light has pierced the darkness,
  As so many times before!

Would you hear the legend's moral?
  We may find one—you and I.
Let us love as Hinemoa,
  Or the strong Tutanekai!

THE TALE OF A LADIES' MAN

HE used to sit in a gilded p'ram,
Hugging a wonderful woolly lamb,
While he fondly grinned at his love, serene,
In a p'ram which was painted a gorgeous green ;
And he yelled in his own peculiar way
(Though nobody guessed what he tried to say),
   " I've found her, boo ! hoo ! I've found her ! "

To school in time he was duly sent
(I believe at the age of ten he went).
He sent many a note and many a box
Of sweets and Parisian creamy choc's
To a Miss at the Girls' Academy,
While he cried to his chums, half mad with glee,
   " I've found her, you chaps, I've found her ! "

As a youth his life was careless and gay
(A little bit fast, so they used to say),
After hundreds of maidens he merrily ran,
And was known as " a regular ladies' man ; "
But he said to himself of each Venus fair,
As he gazed in her eyes with a love-sick stare,
   " I've found her, by Jove ! I've found her ! "

He married a lady exceedingly " smart,"
Who by many a wile laid siege to his heart,
He endured fifteen years of connubial life,
Fifteen years of sorrow and bickering strife ;
And things kept on getting from bad to worse,
Till at last he cried, " What a terrible curse
   I've found her, great Scot ! I've found her !"

But when she left him a widower, free,
Another lady he chanced to see,
A nice little woman (age thirty-five),
Who was not too dull or too much alive.
And he often whispers, when joys are rife,
As he holds the hand of his dear little wife,
   " I've found her, thank God ! I've found her !"

TO A YOUNG LOVER

On discovering with Regret the Humanity of his Lady

ANGELS do not dwell on earth,
　　Far too happy they in heaven!
Would you have an angel-bride?
　　Such to mortals are not given.

Angels never mortals wed,
　　Which is just as it should be,
For I'm sure such different minds
　　Never, never would agree.

You may wed a mortal bride,
　　And, when married life begins,
Possibly you'll love the most
　　Just her little human sins!

WRITTEN FOR MADAME MARIE VANTINI'S
ALBUM

THE PROPHECY

PENELOPE and I, at shadow-time,
　　Went to a gipsy-prophetess, who said
That ere another year had passed away
　　We both of us most surely would be wed.

Penelope said coyly, with a smile,
　　She wondered who the lucky man would be,
And I declared I did not know the girl
　　Who ever could be good enough for me.

But then she blushed, and I said many things
　　(Things which I will not now repeat to you !)
And as we wandered back, through leafy lanes,
　　We thought the gipsy's prophecy was true.

THREE GIRLS

I.—THE BABY-GIRL

SHE entered the world in sorrow, for scarcely had she come into the dark room, with the drawn curtains and the anxious muffled voices, before Death followed and took from her in one short moment all the joy and love which are expressed by the word "mother."

She was a sadly weak baby. Nature is kind in such matters, and in after-years she remembered little of her childhood—little except the kindness of a good old soul, who was her nurse, and the love which her father had towards his child, also the kindness of the "dear, kind lady" concerning whom you shall hear more anon.

The old nurse now lives in a beautiful cottage in Westmoreland—rather like the quaint cottage of Anne Hathaway—covered in summer-time with roses and honeysuckle. Her greatest pleasures in life are occasional visits from the girl she loves as her own child.

The baby-girl was very pretty. In her white linen she looked like a little cherub, with a dimple in her cheek and a rather pathetic smile.

She was unlike other baby-girls in being so very, very good, which, in babies, means so very, very quiet.

Some one once said of her that " she was always seeing visions of heaven ; " and this described her very well.

At his club her father's friends whispered among themselves a good deal after her entrance in life's drama. There was plenty of honest, manly sympathy, and the baby-girl at an absurdly early age made the acquaintance of several elderly gentlemen and several very nice boys.

Her father was young and very handsome, but his wife's death, as his friends whispered among themselves, seemed to have aged him many years in a few weeks. His only comfort was the baby-girl. He gazed at her with tears in his fine eyes, with a strange mixture of love and fear—for no man has ever yet absolutely understood a baby !

He would sit beside her for hours because she reminded him of the " dear, dead woman," and when the old nurse came, he would often come into the nursery, for the very atmosphere of the baby-girl's own room seemed alone to cheer him in those dark days.

She looked at him in her strange way, and sometimes would coo with pleasure and laugh at him until he stroked her tiny head and laughed himself like a schoolboy.

Years passed and the baby-girl grew stronger and a little more bewitching every day. She was a very beautiful child, with long wavy curls and a pair of

peerless little hands.   As she grew older her love for
" daddy " became greater every minute of every day.
She was named Gladys, and seemed a little sunbeam
sent to cheer the life of a very sad young man.

She had many admirers.   Not only the grim old
men at the club, who, if the truth be told, terrified
her slightly with their strong cigars, their gruff voices,
and their fat fingers with which they invariably chucked
her under her chubby little chin, but also tall beautiful
ladies, with sweet faces and silvery voices, who loved
the lonely little child, and took her to see their own
children, so that she might not be without friends.

Yet she was always glad to get back to " daddy,"
who was nicer than all the children in the world.

Among her admirers was one lady she loved most
of all, whom she called the " dear, kind lady."

She saw her first at a children's party, and sat on
her knee a long while listening to wonderful stories,
including one very beautiful one about a poor, lonely
old man, called a merman, whose wife had left him
all alone with his children on the shore.

When the tale was told both were crying, and the
lady kissed her and said they must find the other
people, who would be wondering what had become of
them, and that they must see each other often again.

They often did meet.   Gladys used to go to the
lady's pretty house and stay there for hours playing
with Toby, a pug who soon became one of her greatest
friends, listening to wonderful stories which the lady
told her in a voice full of tears, like the beautiful

voice of Mrs. Patrick Campbell, building houses with bricks or looking at books with coloured pictures.

Soon, moreover, daddy also came often to see the " dear, kind lady " (with the old nurse as chaperone !), and then one day Gladys was told to call the " dear, kind lady ' mamma !'"

At the club they laughed, and, in presenting the bride and bridegroom with a pair of carvers, said " the kiddie was the youngest match-maker in the world."

Yet she was also the golden thread which was to bind two loving hearts together.

So, at first hardly understanding why, Gladys called the " dear, kind lady ' mamma !'"

II.—THE CLEVER GIRL

SHE was not really very clever, but when men or women shut themselves up with books written in dead languages and work very, very hard, they are apt to have this adjective applied to them—it proved so in her case.

She had lived in a grey, old country vicarage, in that pure, sunny atmosphere of simple piety which is so precious, she was the idol of old villagers—" the parson's daughter."

Then had come sorrow—the death of her parents,

a dishonest lawyer, and the awful necessity of facing the world alone.

The situation was not new—she was in the position of so many girls in the books she had read in the hammock in the orchard. They had all faced the world and won; she determined to face the world— and trust the future to God !

She was not pretty, she was very quiet and fond of little children, she loved poetry, and all animals were her friends. She was never so happy as when reading, or petting some great dog or peevish little child or some sad old body who loved to talk of her rheumatics and her grandchildren !

So she determined to become a governess. She would have children to teach, and she would have books. But soon she found there were so sadly few people in the world who needed governesses; moreover, they wanted a girl to know so much—French and Latin, and sometimes even Greek, to say nothing of piano-playing.

So, quite alone, she determined to shut herself up and learn.

She hired a small room which contained a tin-kettley piano, bought dictionaries and grammars, collected some of her father's old books, and sat down a student.

Then people began to call her a clever girl. She now laughed at herself for presuming to offer to teach when she was such an ignoramus.

Her ignorance was the nightmare of her life, and

she worked far into the nights, till her eyes ached and filled with tears of wild despair.

"Oh, why am I such an ignorant, useless fool?" she moaned to herself; and in bed she would dream that angels put on her poor tired brow the laurel-wreath of wisdom, that the wise men of all ages, led by Solomon, came to consult her on all kinds of subjects, and that she gave answers which were taken down in a new " Book of Proverbs " not yet given to the world.

But in the morning the cold, grey light entered, lighting up the small crucifix on her mantelpiece, and the dismal reality faced her once more.

So she would practise scales and spell out dreadful Latin books, and so on for days and weeks.

Then she entered for examinations and passed. People said still she was a clever girl, and the words were spoken half-scornfully, for clever girls are not sometimes over-popular.

She soon took to spectacles, and then queer old-maidish habits came upon her which she half smiled at to herself, and she became absent-minded and a little less kind to those she met—the poor and sad—not because she really loved them less, but because she was so busy, and her mind was full of strange distracting things—above all, anxiety to learn.

Then she died—very suddenly—and they found her one morning clasping the crucifix in her hands, looking very weary, her hair just a trifle grey, and by her bedside a small volume of Horace's Odes.

The room was very bare, and the only picture was one of her father and an old dog—a photograph she had taken once in life's sunshine.

So ends the story of the clever girl.

III.—THE SINGING GIRL

with some account of

"THE DEAR GOOD BOYS"

THERE is a small flat, very high up, not far from the venerable and highly respectable Exhibition of Madame Tussaud, which was once honoured by the presence of a fairy singer.

The girl of whom I write must have been a fairy, she was so unlike many London girls. The Fates had given her much beauty and an enchanting voice which made all who heard it dream of goodness; yet she was neither conceited, affectedly modest, nor aggressively independent.

She dressed very simply, yet she always appeared in some mysterious way better dressed than any one else, and a small leather music-case tucked under her arm declared to passers-by the fact of which she was prouder than of anything else—that she belonged to the very noble and very delightful army of "the girls who work."

She might best be described as full of charm.   Her life was very happy, for although she worked hard her work was the greatest joy of her life, and she was loved by all who knew her, who taught her, or who listened to her; also she loved everybody in return very much; and to love and be loved is great happiness to any girl.

Love of work, and especially of art-work, makes a girl so much more charming, so much more possible, so much more REAL, than love of that petty existence misnamed "society"—whether it be in Brixton or Park Lane.

In love of art lies salvation for duchesses and shop-girls, and dukes and shopmen alike.

Little girls in brown (or big girls in any other colour for that matter; but I notice that so many of them are little girls in brown or black!), with happy mouths, and bright, soulful eyes, and voices full of joy; and dear, vivacious manners which English-people generally describe as "so French" (*vive l'entente cordiale!*); and minds full of sunshine, which is the purging sunshine of knowledge,—ever seem to me the salt of the earth.   And the Fairy was one of them.   Such girls are not always pretty, but they are always full of charm, which is so much better.

Many of them are to be found in the region of Queen's Hall, which some may say goes to prove that music is the greatest of the arts!

Among the staunchest admirers of the Fairy was a *coiffeur*, who was alone permitted to make more beautiful her beautiful hair—a commission almost as precious as Royal patronage !

His *salon* contained countless queer-shaped phials of glass, in which were frictions with strange names and wonderful colours—like liqueurs—which soothed tired heads on the dreariest days.

There was also a hairwash invented by himself, of which he was justly proud—it was as the foam of the sea—a greenish-blue hairwash, meet for mermaids to bathe in !

And in his *salon* was almost every kind of perfume : simple perfumes, which caused one to think of country lanes and fresh country maidens and pretty weddings in little churches nestling in green valleys, conducted by parsons whom Dickens would have loved ; heavy sensuous perfumes from the East, which conjured up pictures of rich tapestries and soft couches, and dancing-girls clashing cymbals above their heads, and incense burning in bronze bowls, and palaces glistening with precious stones ; delicate, plaintive perfumes, like some melody of Schubert, or the " Rosen aus dem Süden " of Strauss, which set one thinking of hearts throbbing for love's sacred sorrow, of lovers gazing by moonlight across some sapphire sea, dreaming, dreaming, dreaming of the impossible—man's eternal goal, which is the more precious because it is never reached ; frivolous perfumes, which suggested laughter and sparkling wine and sparkling eyes, and an orchestra

C

playing musical comedy, and the glad, mad folly of the *demi-monde;* cheap scents for the cheap flirtations of *Boul' Mich' belles;* perfumes meet for duchesses when they sat at dinner with the king; and perfumes meet for Ninon, or Mimi, or Céleste, or any other little *grisette* from the Latin quarter, when she sat with Alphonse or any other good Bohemian at the *Closerie des Lilas*, enjoying *Vin* (very) *ordinaire* and a cigarette!

Every perfume has some hidden story, sometimes a romance, sometimes—well! rather "blue"—sometimes a tale of heart-sorrow, sometimes a tale so full of joy that one feels the joy cannot last, but must in time give place to sorrow all the greater because of contrast.

A *coiffeur* is indeed a privileged person sometimes, and his is a romantic profession—the preservation of youth and beauty. Not that the Fairy needed any "preservation," you may be sure!

He is also privileged because from those magic perfume-bottles he pours forth dreams and hidden stories which only dreamers may discover—emotions, tears, laughter, good, evil. He is an apothecary for the soul!

I often think that flowers, poems, liqueurs, and perfumes should be sold only by Beauty's children.

One can buy a cabbage from a coster without pain, but to buy Shelley's poems from a Nonconformist "light" is a sad experience, yet a frequent one!

Flowers one would like to purchase from some tall lady, with dark hair and eyes, and long delicate

fingers—a Rossetti maiden, or some lady such as
Du Maurier might have drawn, or like Whistler's
"Princesse du pays de la Porcelaine."

She would bring us pale lilies and roses of wondrous
tints, and violets whose scent recalls the music of an
old-world minuet, and all the flowers would seem to us
the fairer for remembrance of her ; and when we gave
them to the girls we loved we should whisper to ourselves that there is always room for beauty in our
imperfect world !

To sell poems I think one would choose beautiful
youths with red lips and perfumed hair—reincarna-
tions of the Elgin Marbles—youths who still stand
wondering at life, and who live not in the world
which sneers at beauty, but in the far better world
of Keats and Wagner and all the immortals.

No one should ever spoil them by telling them that
they were "artistic" or "unlike most people"—all
too soon would they find out that ! they would be
natural, and therefore truly unconventional, acolytes as
it were in the Temple of Beauty, and with pure white
hands should they touch lovingly and with awe the
books which are among the sacred things of the world
—the books of those who strive nobly, as well as of
those who succeed.

If, as the years rolled by, they were still undefiled
—if they never lost their ideals—the acolytes should
become priests, that is to say, booksellers or authors,
who strive for beauty rather than for gold.

Liqueurs should be sold in my ideal country by

little wise old men, who should sit at the doors of quaint shops full of fascinating phials.

They would know that liqueurs are not intended to quench thirst, but rather to soothe or to inspire the soul, and to them would come the sad to be comforted, and the seekers after beauty for new thoughts.

They would resemble Shakespeare's apothecary and Friar Lawrence rolled into one, but much cleaner, full of humanity and kindness, and at little tables outside their shops men and women should drink, and, while some forgot their sorrows, others should find new and unexpected joys, and all should be truly born again.

In the sunlight or the moonlight should glisten tiny goblets filled with colours—*amer picon, sirop d'orgeat, Benedictine, crème de menthe, maraschino, anisette, Chartreuse,* "*angels' tears,*" and countless others, like fairy lamps, but far more beautiful.

It would seem as if little unseen sprites sat on the rims of the glasses and poured thoughts into the glittering bowls, and many should come to live again with dead people whom they loved, and in fancy once again would they hold thin hands, and once again gaze into well-loved eyes. And the unseen sprites would smile and pass on to give other thoughts to other folk—thoughts of lovers to waiting maidens, thoughts of fame to starving poets, thoughts of riches to the poor, and perhaps thoughts of comfortable poverty to the rich, who desired no greater blessing !

And on the glasses, in small letters of gold, should be these words—

"The soul is but the senses catching fire,
Marvellous music of the body's lyre
The angel-senses are the silver strings
Stirred by the breath of some unknown desire."

All who frequented these little shops would know their OMAR very well.

And perfumes? Well, I would allow perfumes to be sold by all *coiffeurs* who had a sense of beauty, such as the admirer of our Fairy; and by all who were lonely and who lived in a world of yesterday; for are not perfumes liquid memories, thoughts materialized as it were for the use of those who need them?

Their *salons* would, of course, be open to all, and perhaps one would come for *eau de violette*, because "it recalls a summer afternoon on the river fifteen years ago;" or another would crave some peculiar scent of the East, which should recall thoughts of a secret love, just as music brings to life dead days; or others not yet old enough to have many memories would ask for "Jockey Club," "because Ralph loves it so," or for some other perfume which "I always wear when Vivien reads me his verses or plays his music;" or those whom the Japanese have beautifully named "mournful sisters of joy" would buy scents which half please half nauseate, as the false fervours of false "love;" and as there would be scents which should remind, so should others teach how to forget!

Ah, yes! all this would be better, far better, than buying flowers from unromantic charwomen, and poems from the Nonconformist "light," and liqueurs from some soulless son of Israel with a large belly and rings of fat and of diamonds, and perfumes from a grocer "much respected in Upper Tooting" (*vide* local papers, if there are any). But, like so many joyous things, it may not be.

Oh that even for one little day life and art might again be synonymous terms, as in ancient Greece! A Grecian day would be worth many British years!

The Fairy was the president, or rather the *raison d'être*, as Monsieur Thibault, her singing-master, had told her, of a small and exceedingly select club which she had named " The Dear Good Boys!"

"The Dear Good Boys"—six in number—were all the best of pals, and were all fellow-worshippers of the Fairy.

They were always welcome at the little flat near Madame Tussaud's, which might be described as their club-rooms, and they never failed to pay their voluntary subscriptions, sometimes in sketches from the two artist-members, in poems from the poet, or in gifts of all kinds from the other members, seats for the theatres, flowers, chocolates, cosy little suppers, or concert tickets from poor old Monsieur Thibault —the only gifts he had to give, which she might have obtained for herself, but for which she was always very grateful !

"The Dear Good Boys" were also indefatigable in conducting the Fairy home from her triumphs at the concert-rooms, and many a gilded Johnny has cursed one or other of the members of the club on such occasions.

When the Fairy returned home with her escort, ten to one she would find all the other " Dear Good Boys " waiting for her, except, perhaps, Monsieur Thibault, who would arrive later on, when his conducting was over; and she would retire for a few minutes and then return, having taken off her hat and jacket, and sit down to make coffee in a queer little coffee-pot, and cigarettes would be handed round, pipes lit, drinks brought out, and all preparations made for a club meeting.

Needless to say, the meetings were absolutely informal. There was plenty of laughter and a good deal of real wit inspired by pipes, cigarettes, and drinks, to say nothing of the presence of the Fairy, which was the greatest inspiration of all.

Then there would be music and songs. Monsieur Thibault would be called upon to play " Star of Eve " on his violin, which, with the Fairy's accompaniment, was a musical performance hard to equal; or the poet would sing his own songs, which were criticized, sometimes chaffingly, but never unkindly; or, best of all, the Fairy would sing while Monsieur Thibault played, and tears came into his kind old eyes as he listened to the voice of his pupil.

The poet once wrote some verses, which may be interesting if quoted here. Of course, he dedicated them to the Fairy, and he headed them

"A Fairy's Bower

" Dear little room, with paper blue,
　　With pictures and books and flowers,
Dainty as she who loves them all,
　　Snuggest of fairy bowers.

" Dear little room, with cosy chairs,
　　With quaint little odds and ends,
Photos and ornaments everywhere,
　　Presents from faithful friends.

" Dear little room, where music sounds
　　When the work of day is done,
Where songs are sung, both sad and gay,
　　Beautiful every one.

" Dear little lady, be sure that I
　　Your bower shall ne'er forget,
The prettiest picture in all the world
　　Is you with a cigarette ! "

From which it is revealed that the Fairy smoked,
which I hope will not shock any very genteel readers.
If they had seen her smoking I am sure they would
have agreed with the poet—she smoked because she
enjoyed it, not because she desired to pose, or to
appear " naughty " or " Bohemian "—and it makes
such a difference !

Well! they were all "Dear Good Boys" and very happy, but gradually it became evident that the Fairy considered the poet the dearest and best boy of them all. He never will forget the dear little room or the dear little lady, we may be sure; for the Fairy became his wife.

The other "Dear Good Boys" were regretfully glad. They knew he was a real good fellow; moreover, it was a genuine love match; yet a little regret was only human.

The *coiffeur's* present was a huge bottle of a truly wonderful perfume, which seemed as full of magic as the *Arabian Nights!*

At a supper in the "club-rooms" the evening before the Fairy's wedding-day the gaiety was a little forced. Of course, they said they would all be as great friends as ever; but, as men of the world, they knew things would have to be different.

That night they all kissed the Fairy for the first and last time in their lives—except, of course, the poet!

Then they all felt more regretful than ever, and most of their eyes were moist, while the Fairy sobbed for sorrow mixed with joy.

The next day Monsieur Thibault played the wedding march, one of the artists was best man, and the other "Dear Good Boys" were all present. These were but the formalities of friendship, but the real parting was at that supper in the small flat near Madame Tussaud's.

The flat is still there, but now all its daintiness has

vanished with the Fairy whom the poet has taken with him into the country, and it is inhabited by a religious maniac, who addresses grimy mobs on Sundays and writes tracts all the week.

And as marriage is popularly supposed to change a girl into a woman in the shortest possible space of time, I suppose the tale of the singing *girl* is told.

A CHILD'S SOUL

" . . . To die ; to sleep ;
No more ; and by a sleep to say we end
The heartache, and the thousand natural shocks
That flesh is heir to,—'tis a consummation
Devoutly to be wished."

Hamlet, act iii. sc. 1.

ONCE in a cold, dark street, in winter-time,
There chanced a wondrous meeting.   Life and Death
Strove o'er the body of a little child.
Frozen she lay upon a snow-deck'd stone,
When Death approached, and with his heavy cloak
Touched her the while he stretched a long lean hand
To raise her up and claim her for his own.
Then suddenly he started all amazed,
For at his side appeared the beauteous form
Of Life, as some fair angel, flown from heaven,
And thus addressed her adversary Death :
" Thou King of Darkness, feared by one and all,
Unwelcome, yet most necessary guest,
Now, I implore thee, grant a boon to me—
That this one little maiden shall not die.
See ! she is young, she knows not of the joy

That I can give her as the years roll on.
Thou hast so many victims, I beseech
That thou wilt spare this little tender flower.
Grim tyrant, strike not at an innocent child!
Let pity calm the fury of thy mind,
As music teacheth base men gentleness."
While thus she spake, tears fell from out her eyes
Like sparkling jewels, and the grim old Death
Bent low his shaggy head in humble mien,
Trembling before his fair antagonist.
Then turned to her, and said in hollow voice:
"Thou Queen, beloved of mortals, think not I
Have not a heart and hate not to be feared.
Thou art so happy in the love of men,
Canst thou, dear lady, learn to pity me,
A sad old man, beloved by not one soul?
Unwelcome when I bring the precious gift
Of endless rest which I alone can give.
Think not that I am heedless of the woe
Of women, wailing for their children dead;
Of wives for whom, through me, the world is dark;
Of lovers, who may see no marriage day;
Of broken hearts and weary loneliness
In the stern world of mortals; worst of all,
The stifled sobbing of a strong brave man.
True, I am 'King of Darkness,' yet the balm,
The ending of all sorrow, may be found
In that great darkness which but leads to light.
I give the gift of peace to thankless men,
Who loathe my name and crouch at my approach.

Now do I seek this maiden for mine own—
She shall not know one sorry day nor hour,
But sleep in peace until the end of time,
If she be mine; while, if I take her not,
Leaving her unto thee as thou dost ask,
What sorrow shall she know! what toil and tears!
A childhood lived in never-ending want;
Later perchance a husband's drunken wrath,
The cry of little mouths she cannot fill,
Temptation ever whispering in her ears,
Whispering softly, till in hour of need
Yielding, she lives and dies, perhaps, in shame.
Is it not better if I take her now
To save her from such woeful life as this;
To save her from the sin and cruelty,
The bitterness, which ever comes with life,
That doubtful blessing which 'tis thine to give?
Think not, O Life, that I am always hard.
How often might we twain be dearest friends,
If we might better know each other's ways!"
He ceased; and for a while no sound was heard,
Save the low moaning of the wintry wind.
Then Life stooped down and gently kissed the child,
The little sleeping beauty at her feet,
Who smiled as if she dreamed the happy truth.
Death watched the deed, and with admiring eyes
He gazed at Life, who, coming close to him,
Clasped in her own his trembling bony hands:
"How have I wronged thee, unknown friend!" she
     cried.

" Take thou this child to realms of endless peace.
Gladly I give her to thee : better 'tis
She die in peace than live in cruel want."
Slowly Death bent and kissed her outstretched hand,
Before he took the sleeping little child
Tenderly in his arms and crept away,
While Life gazed after him as in a trance.

A GIRL AND A POET

A LONDON ROMANCE

"Our simple life wants little, and true taste
Hires not the pale drudge Luxury to waste
The scene it would adorn."

Shelley, *Epipsychidion.*

THE poet first saw the girl on a wet afternoon in
Trafalgar Square.

She was alone and, by a merciful providence of
Heaven, without an umbrella.

An idea had come to him suddenly, and, since he
belonged to no club, he had rushed into a post-office
to add it to the MSS. of a poem before handing it
to the editors, who so often in his case did not edit,
but reject.

This sudden birth of ideas is a painful complaint
common among poets, I believe—almost as terrible
as having no ideas at all!

The National Gallery, with its absurd pepper-box,
looked, he thought, more national than ever.

A French *mot* came into his mind, "The English
are never humorous except in Art."

Of course it was untrue, but at the same time it

was rather smart; he would like to have made it himself, and the exterior of the National Gallery was surely the greatest artistic joke.

He felt ashamed of his depression, and, in order to banish it, repeated to himself Emerson's words, "To the Poet:" "Wherever day and night meet in twilight, wherever the blue heaven is hung by clouds or sown with stars, wherever are forms with transparent boundaries, wherever are outlets into celestial space, wherever is danger and awe and love, there is beauty, plenteous as rain, shed for thee, and though thou shouldst walk the world over, thou shalt not be able to find a condition inopportune or ignoble."

It was cheering to think of his inheritance, but, alas! his condition just then was described earlier in the passage, "The world is full of renunciations and apprenticeships, and this is thine; thou must pass for a fool and a churl for a long season. This is the screen and sheath in which Pan has protected his well-beloved flower, and thou shalt be known only to thine own, and they shall console thee with tenderest love."

He had indeed "passed for a fool and a churl," but that "consolation of tenderest love" had not yet been his.

It was to come to him very soon.

Many people politely or impolitely cursed that wet afternoon, but the poet has sung a private song of thanksgiving for it ever since.

Why? Well, because had it not been wet the girl

had had no need of an umbrella, and had she had
no need of an umbrella he had had no opportunity of
taking her under his, and had he not taken her under
his the world would have continued to be for him a
rather dreary place.

More friendships are wrought by umbrellas than
this world dreams of!

The girl was wearing a black dress, a white feather
boa, and a hat daintily trimmed with pink ribbon.

She held her skirt up just sufficiently to show a
small pair of brown shoes, also a pair of brown stock-
ings, and a petticoat which was surely meant to be
seen and admired of all mankind!

Under her arm was tucked a song-case, and she
was getting very, very wet.

The poet caught her up, and presented himself and
his umbrella with a courtly bow.

As they walked together they soon seemed to be
old friends.

He learned that she was an actress, and she learned
his profession, which she had guessed directly she
saw him.

They were both bound to the Strand and Fleet
Street, those battle-fields of Art.

She wished to inquire whether her agent had got
her an engagement; he to dispose, if possible, of
some verses.

They parted at the agent's door, but not, you may
be sure, until they had arranged to meet again later—
at the Café X.

D

When they met again they sat at a little corner table, full of a wonderful joy.

It was seven o'clock in October—a time when, especially in wet weather, London is full of Whistler effects. Through the *café* door could be seen shop-girls—respectable little English *grisettes*—scurrying home to read Marie Corelli or Hall Caine.

The poet's verses were still bulging out of his coat-pocket with a beautiful blueswan quill, and the girl had once more heard that old cry, " Nothing for you yet, my dear; call again in a day or two." But their misfortunes only seemed to make them better friends. The poet, poor fellow ! had one of the largest collections of " returned-with-thanks " forms in the world !

That was the first of many suppers. They met every night, and when the girl went on tour she always found her poet waiting anxiously for her on her return.

They always sat at the corner table, and the waiters would have done anything for them, I believe—perhaps even have given them free suppers, had it been in their power to do so !

They were from sunny Italy, you see, and, I think, most Italians know by instinct a good deal about poetry and love !

They always preferred English customers to speak their mother tongue, which they understood far better than the usual English-French, which is confined to " Garsong," and mispronunciation of the *menu !*

After supper, coffee and cigarettes at one of the

larger *cafés* were very pleasant—nearly always at Frascati's, for there was to be heard an enchanting orchestra, with a violinist greatly gifted by the gods.

The black gentleman, with red cap and uniform of gold and green, who with much appropriate ritual manufactured Turkish coffee, in fascinating little cups, was a great friend of theirs.

There can be no more delightful place in which to study life than a *café;* it is so much less draughty than a railway station!

How interesting are the artists, the lovers, the social outcasts, yes, even the British vulgarians trying to be " gay "—half-dead people endeavouring to be too much alive!

A *Café Gazette* would be an interesting periodical; it would soon supplant those society journals which tell us everything people are *not* doing in town!

A *café* is almost as enchanting as a toy-shop, and, after all, is it not a kind of toy-shop on the *boulevard* of Life?—a toy-shop very full of dolls.

The girl and the poet talked to each other of all sorts of things—all the new plays, Keats, Shakespeare, a national theatre, Maeterlinck, Ibsen, and other subjects, which were, of course, links in the chain which bound these souls together, and both lived in a world which seemed like heaven and Fairyland in one.

They often went to pits together (they had no dress clothes in those days for the stalls!), and once when they had sat spellbound at *Tannhäuser*, that wonderful human story of life and death, sorrow and love, the poet told the secret of his heart, which was no revelation to the girl !

As they walked beneath the stars that night to the little *café*, they were too happy to speak ; but at supper they pretended they were host and hostess at a large dinner-party given to all the brilliant people in literature and drama. "Mr. Harvey, do let me give you some more partridge," said the girl, slipping *poulet roti* upon the poet's plate, and the poet made himself very charming to Mrs. Humphry Ward.

Thus they enjoyed to the full the divine silliness of love.

And at Frascati's that night the orchestra played "The Wedding March," which I suppose was "just a curious coincidence, and nothing more."

We are so unwilling to admit that unknown powers ever affect our lives, or that Fate ever plays little tricks like this upon us by way of reminding us that we are as marionettes dangling from a string in the hands of THE UNKNOWN !

The poet drove the girl home in a hansom—an unprecedented luxury—but was not this an unprecedented night ?

The romance and fascination of hansoms will never be destroyed. Vain efforts have been made to do so, as when somebody called them "the gondolas of London ;" but all to no avail.

How the girl and the poet kissed, and laughed, and sighed, and nestled together as they drove down the avenue of lights, which seemed as if it might lead to some land of eternal joy, let all lovers picture for themselves.

There were no horrible flaring looking-glasses in that hansom, the horse had no past, and the driver was sympathetic—a jovial cabby with a large button-hole.

Jangle, jangle, jangle, went the bells.

The poet wondered whether this cab had carried many lovers before. It had probably done so, for the driver seemed quite conscious of the situation.

Also, of course, it had carried unhappy little beggars on their way back to school, and happy little beggars home from school as well !

And beautiful ladies had driven in it, and people perhaps had sighed and wept in it, and formed great plans in it, and driven in it to see their lovers or to see their dead.

Or perhaps once it had been honoured by that great strange poet whose delight was to ride in a hansom all day, after purchasing beautiful flowers for his driver and himself ! Who could tell ? The confessions of a hansom might be as interesting as those of a *grande dame.* It would tell tales of early morning and late night, tales of folly, tales of sorrow and of joy. Yes ! perhaps one day he might write *Confessions of a Hansom Cab !* It should, of course, be dedicated " To my Wife," and it should be beautifully bound in green and gold.

They drove along the Cromwell Road, and the poet thought what great comfort its awful sternness must bring its patron, who probably sadly needed a little comfort now and then !

When at last this wonderful drive was over, and the horse stopped before the girl's humble little lodging, there were tears in her eyes; but as the poet kissed her he knew that they were not tears of sorrow, but tears of joy too great for the heart to hold.

And the cabby never asked for an extra sixpence !

Perhaps he also had once been poor and very much in love !

The poet, as he walked home alone, met a blind man.

Nearer and nearer came the slow, even tapping of his stick upon the pavement—a sound full of hopeless sorrow.

Into his hand the poet pressed two shillings.

It was a night of wild expense, of reckless joy.

A drunken minstrel carrying a banjo, whose blackened face accentuated the whiteness of his trousers and the tawdry patchwork of his waistcoat, cursed him as a fool.

And so he was—a fool intoxicated with the glad wisdom of his folly !

Looking back, he saw the blind man and the minstrel arm-in-arm; above them shone the moon, causing the banjo to glitter in the darkness.

A large black cat darted between the minstrel's legs.

The whole scene was of the impressionist school !

Of course a barrel-organ accompaniment would

have been an improvement; but it was too late at night for that!

* * * * *

All this happened a year ago, and this London romance is now being continued in a snug little flat in Hampstead, where the girl and the poet are living two of the simplest, happiest lives in all the world.

Success is slowly coming to them both.

Before we leave them I would like to mention two of their peculiarities.

The first is their devotion to a corner table in a rather shabby little *café;* the second, a curious custom of theirs never to complain of rain!

You see, they have always sunshine in their hearts.

VERSES TO A DEAD GIRL

I

AT that hushed time when light and darkness mix,
  I saw thee gazing far across the sea.
  Dear heart, before my eyes there seemed to be
A vision of "Beata Beatrix."

Dear heart, I watched thee once, and thou didst seem,
  As I methinks have often seen thee look
  When reading from some loved immortal book,
Half-angel, wondering there at " Dante's Dream."

And once I saw thee when the daylight died,
  In church, thy face lit with a holy joy,
  Sobbing beside a little orphan boy,
Who knelt in prayer to Jesus crucified.

II

I came to you when summer roses grew
  Around the porch, and 'neath the winding stair
A vase of honeysuckle welcomed me.
  You were most welcome of all flowers there !

I came to you again in winter-time.
   We both were throbbing with a dim desire.
As in the firelight soul spoke forth to soul,
   Your heart was warmer than the glowing fire !

I saw you in your dainty coffin-bed,
   I knelt beside you full of mystic fear,
I kissed you while I sobbed—then knew, O God !
   Your cheeks were colder than friends' comfort, dear.

III

Sometimes when moonlight falls upon the sea,
   I think of scenes and friends in days gone by.
Once more I gaze upon my little love,
   Of whom I may not think without a sigh.

She came to me like some enchanting dream.
   My loving vows had scarce to her been given,
When from my arms, which fain would clasp her yet,
   Her fairy soul flew home again to heaven.

Sometimes when church-bells sound at eventide,
   And all is very beautiful and still,
I think I hear her singing plaintive songs,
   My lonely heart with ecstasy to fill.

"THE LAST GRIM JOKE"

"SELFISHNESS personified."

Thus a tame humourist had described the cynic to some fellow-humourists yet tamer than himself, on the way from dining at the cynic's expense.

The fellow-humourists firmly believed that their leader had made a smart remark!

Meanwhile the cynic sat before his fire, bemoaning to himself the excruciating mildness of everything.

His rooms were an armoury of weapons for use against the fiend Boredom. New novels, new papers, photos of new girls were scattered about; but the fiend had broken through the defence, and the cynic was asking for terms of surrender.

He had reached the stage of cynicism at which there is no use for any being or thing in the wide world save as a target for a sneer—the last stage of all.

During his short life, Joy had given him every gift she had to give, and he had cast all her gifts away—he realized with terror that he could never be really happy again.

He sat very still gazing into the flames—a young, old man.

Then Death came and stood beside his chair.

"Would you like to die?" said Death, and touched his shoulder with a bony hand.

The cynic laughed. "My dear sir," he said, "I owe you a deep debt of gratitude. You have surprised me by your appearance here, and I have not been genuinely surprised for I dare not say how many dreary years.—Die? It will be a new sensation at last. Yes, I would rather like to die."

So he died, and the most tragic thing about the whole affair was that no one missed him very much.

But the tame humourist attended the funeral with his fellow-humourists yet tamer than himself, and they had the good taste to refrain from making a joke on the occasion.

The only tears were shed by the newest girl.

CONCERNING A LITERARY GENTLEMAN AND A SPIRIT

THE literary gentleman sat at his writing-desk, wearing a troubled look (*et cetera !*).

He nibbled a quill pen and passed long fingers through rough hair. He was endeavouring to produce something original.

The waste-paper basket was stuffed with many extremely ordinary storyettes, some humorous verses, which were rather more humorous than they were ever intended to be, and some essays setting forth the ordinary young man's views of a very old world.

He had hurled them away because they were all old subjects with new titles. Some brightly coloured caricatures of poems had just met with the same fate. The literary gentleman was inwardly cursing Mr. Max Beerbohm.

The bust of Shakespeare before him gave no inspiration, the portrait of Hall Caine " at home " gave no comfort. Shelley still looked like a frightened fawn, and Penley still grinned inanely as Charley's aunt.

Oh, for originality ! He dropped the pen and lit his meerschaum.

Wreaths of smoke filled the room. Hall Caine, Shelley, and Penley disappeared ; finally Shakespeare also was lost to view.

The literary gentleman found himself muttering that originality was impossible ; " original " writers were merely those who wrote on old subjects in a new manner—for instance, Mr. Barrie and his dramatic treatise on the stomach ! or the chirpy philosophy of Mr. Chesterton.

Then appeared to him the Spirit of Originality.

She looked like a fairy from Drury Lane, and spoke like a school-child reciting for a piece of toffee.

The literary gentleman thought vaguely of Charles Hawtrey and " The Message from Mars."

" *Write the truth*," she said, and vanished with a wave of a twopenny wand.

He wrote it, and became one of the most original authors in the world !

FIRELIGHT SONG

Say, little girl, do you love me
    As we sit in the firelight glow?
Say, little girl, do you love me?
    For I want so much to know.
Say, do you love me truly,
    Say, do you love me well?
As I gaze in your wonderful eyes, dear,
    I think I can almost tell.

Say, little girl, are you ready
    To face the whole world with me?
To share all my pleasures and sorrows,
    The queen of my life to be?
Say, little girl, will you wed me?
    For I love you with all my heart;
As a blind man praying for eyesight,
    So I pray we may never part.

TO FREDA AND THELMA

A CREATION LEGEND

GOD yearned a wondrous world to make,
The atoms in His mighty hands to take,
His best to do for every creature's sake.

Earth groaned in bitter misery,
Praying in solemn stillness to the sea
That light as well as darkness there might be.

Sun smiled upon the world new-made.
Then trees and countless flowers themselves displayed,
The smiling summons Nature soon obeyed.

Flowers pined for flatterers and friends,
So Man and Woman came to make amends,
(And with them all the strife which never ends !)

IN THE STUDIO

SUGGESTED BY L. BALESTRIER'S PICTURE
" BEETHOVEN "

WITHIN the studio an old man plays
   Beethoven: While the moonlight sheds a glow
   Upon his silvered hair and quivering bow,
Around him flit the ghosts of far-off days.

Sophie accompanies.   Young Louis there
   Stands smoking.   When the wondrous strains begin
   He half·repents of every strange, sad sin,
While Hope o'er-triumphs desolate Despair.

Babette on Carlo's shoulder leans her head,
   Dreaming of love and wild Bohemian joys,
   Of kindly hearts and many dear, good boys,
Shrinking from Age, who comes with noiseless tread.

Old Carlo thinks of life in sunny Spain,
   Of that glad day when he will gaily ride
   Home to his village with a fairy bride,
Babette and he shall never part again.

Near them sits Frank—his wont the world to roam,
   Yet now his head is buried in his hands,
   He sighs for distant friends and distant lands,
A little sister and an English home.

While Rupert, of the brave undaunted heart,
   Thinks of the victories he means to win
   (How happy they who with great aims begin !)
Of vast and still unconquered worlds of Art.

A new-born strength to every heart is given,
   Strange rays light up the studies on the wall,
   A knowledge rests within the souls of all
That earth is nearer than some think to heaven.

E

TO ISABEL

THE STORY OF MÉLITA

ALL the flowers loved Mélita. The trees whispered their secrets to her, the river sparkled gladly in the sunshine as she walked beside the bank.

When she came forth the birds sang happy songs, for they also loved her.

Sometimes she would come forth alone, her great eyes full of joyous wonder at the beauty of life; she would listen to the singing of the birds, her bosom throbbing with pleasure, and, seeing the lovely flowers around her, she would bury her face in them.

Sometimes she would come forth with little laughing children all around her. They would bring her flowers—the flowers longed to be gathered by children's rosy fingers for Mélita—and dance gaily while the river murmured to the flowers, " How happy is our lady to-day ! " then rather sadly, " How long will it last ? " for the river was something of a philosopher. The flowers only whispered, " Always, always," for they were very young and ignorant of everything save joy and beauty.

Sometimes Mélita would come forth reading a book of poems, and there would be tears in her eyes—tears of pity for those who had suffered long ago—so she would lie down and gaze long into the water-mirror, thinking of their sorrow, and dreaming dimly of love, that strange thing which seemed to rule the world, and slowly she would feel herself aglow once more with the joy of living, and would smile.

But the river was anxious, for he knew that when she dreamed of love she thought not of the love of birds and flowers, or of the gentle moon, or of himself, but of the love of men.

Once when Mélita had gone he cried to the sun, "How I love our lady!" and the birds overhearing him sang, "So do we all."

There was silence for a while until the river cried, "May no harm ever come to our dear lady!" The sun only smiled, for he does not know sorrow.

(This is as it should be, for were he to know of all the sins and sorrows of the world his tears would prevent his ever shining very brightly again.)

But the birds knew of the cruelty of men, and sighed as they sang to Mélita on her homeward way.

When the river whispered his fear to the trees, they understood him, for they were some of them very old, and had looked on sad scenes long ago—as most old trees have.

For many weeks Mélita never came near the river.

There was much sorrow, for the birds and trees missed her terribly, and the world seemed empty.

Then one evening her friend, the gentle moon, came to them and whispered, "Look! she comes— our dear lady," then rather sadly, "but not alone."

The birds and the flowers and the trees called to the river, and the river called back to them, "She is really, really coming."

They all gazed on her, and she seemed a little altered—she was mysterious, and smiled almost weirdly upon them. By her side walked a man, and the river whispered to the moon, "What has come to our lady? she seems so changed." "Sorrow," softly answered the moon, for she knows all about sorrow— all about sorrow and love.

The river and the trees were very silent. Mélita lay down beside the man and gazed into his eyes, as once she had gazed into the river, only far more timidly; then he kissed her very often and clasped her in his arms, holding her very close to his side, yet she seemed to be shrinking from him all the while.

The river and the trees did not like him, and when he looked at Mélita his eyes terrified the flowers.

When he had led Mélita away they murmured long together, and an unknown sorrow caused the young flowers to weep for the first time in their lives.

Then one day Mélita came to the river all alone, as she so often used to do.

The sun smiled on her, for although he does not know sorrow he smiles on all the world, and is a comforter, without knowing it, to many weary hearts.

She nestled down among the flowers and seemed to

love them more than she had ever done before; then she looked upon the trees and the birds and the sun; finally, she bent over the river and murmured between great sobs, "Good-bye, dear trees, dear, dear river, dear little flowers, you will never see me again; good-bye, dear birds, you will still sing, but not to me, unless you fly to me in a distant land; only you, dear sun, will still be with me, you and the gentle moon and the holy little stars—'forget-me-nots of the angels.'

"I am going to leave you, to marry one I do not love.

"Ah! you cannot tell, dear, happy little flowers, what it is to marry for gold, not love, to prevent causing those who are dear to one to suffer. I never knew until two short weeks ago; but I shall always love you—you and the river and the trees and the birds—only you; and when I see the sun and the moon, I will send you messages by them, for I know they love me as I love them, and will do all I ask."

She went away still sobbing. A little green-covered book lay by the river, which she had forgotten to take with her.

There was a dreadful silence—a silence as of broken hearts, as of the unshed tears of a strong man in misery.

The river spoke first, "This must not be;" then the trees whispered, "This must not be;" and the old trees murmured, "This is how all the other sorrows came about which we saw long years ago, but it must not be now;" and the flowers sighed, "Our Mélita, our dear lady must not suffer"—they could scarcely say it for grief; and the birds ceased to sing, and sat full of sorrow on the branches of the trees.

Only the sun was calm; he left them to their grief, for he could only smile, and he felt his smiling was out of place!

* * * * *

In the evening they told their sorrow to the moon and stars, and once more the silence of grief fell all around.

Soon the man came along the river-side. He seemed angry; and when he saw the green-covered book, he opened it and frowned, then placed it in his pocket.

He stumbled over the root of an old tree, and fell into the surging river with an oath.

No one heard him.

The silence of death was terrible.

* * * * *

Mélita understood all when the river told her, and knew that he and the old tree had saved her soul.

So the flowers and the birds rejoice again with the river and the trees, for Mélita is theirs as of old, loving and loved; and the sun, who knows not sorrow, still smiles, until the gentle moon, who knows all about sorrow and love, with her attendants, the stars, takes his place.

THE BOWL OF THOUGHTS

To a concert-room an angel came,
  God sent her to earth again,
Into a beautiful golden bowl
  To gather the thoughts of men.

Now, some of the thoughts were like priceless gems,
  Thoughts of purity.
Loving thoughts for those far away,
  Heart-sighs across the sea.

Some of the thoughts were like fairy flowers,
  Thoughts of days gone by,
Blessèd memories summoned forth
  By the music's harmony.

While other thoughts were like drops of dew,
  The tears of hearts that break;
But the evil thoughts of an evil man
  Took the form of a hideous snake.

A BUTTON-HOLE

FLOWERS you gave me when I came away,
   And how I loved them you alone may guess;
Each fairy petal, beautiful and gay,
   Reminded me of your own loveliness.

I will not keep them when in time they die:
   "Your love is ended," they would seem to say.
I'll cast them from me (not without a sigh!),
   And hope for other flowers some future day.

A SILVER RING

A SOULFUL girl once fell in love with Art,
   She bought herself a little silver ring,
And set it on her finger as a sign
   That everything but Art away she'd fling.

She wears that ring at present night and day,
   Yet often by her laughing friends she's told
That soon a lover's "art" will cast its spell
   And turn the little silver ring to gold!

ONE OF GOD'S CHILDREN

THOU gentle child of God, yet strong as steel,
As in the grey old church you meekly kneel,
Methinks I see pure angels round thy head,
And strange wan faces of the holy dead.

They say a soulless lady " wrecked " thy life,
So thou didst leave the din and cruel strife
Of earthly things to live in holy calm
A priest, a saviour of sad souls from harm.

Yet did she wreck thy life?   Ah ! who dare say?
High God shall tell us on the judgment-day.
The saints with Blessèd Mary will be there,
And she who brought thee all thy heart's despair.

Methinks she will be blamed for every wrong
She did thee.   Then will rise an angel-song
Of glad thanksgiving, and the cause that she
Hath saved thy soul from earth-born vanity.

For little children love thee everywhere,
While men and women wracked with wild despair
By thee are led to gaze awhile on heaven.
To God and weary ones thy life is given.

THE PRESENCE

THE man sat alone reading.

Outside, rain had ceased. He could hear the slow drip, drip of water from the roof,—"the wind at his prayers;" the grim whispering of tall trees.

He rose, stepped across to the latticed window, and, opening it, looked out upon the night. The air seemed full of hushed voices craving silence.

He closed the window, lit a pipe, and sat down before the fire—his soul was full of strange fear.

After a while the candle, by the light of which he had been reading, fell to the floor. The fire cast weird shadows which hovered around his chair.

He gazed into the burning coals, seeing visions there—the meadow in which he first saw the girl he loved, lanes in which he whispered to her over and over again

    " That short, sweet song, whose echo clear,
      Will last throughout eternity,
     'I love thee! How I love thee!'"

It was raining again. Still the wailing wind was praying to the sky.

He was shuddering at the dim light, the shadows, a mysterious Presence which he could not see, yet he dared not strike a match.

He stirred the fire, and again gazed into the flames.

The coals moved, and the sound shot terror through him; he felt he was not alone, beads of sweat were on his brow.

In the fire he saw a small coffin decked with flowers, beside which he knelt, sobbing wildly. Slowly he recognized the scene: it was *her* room, and there hanging on the door were her little blue jacket and straw hat.

He looked on calmly, scarcely realizing, yet longing to see all.

He sat quite still. His pipe was out long ago, but he held it listlessly in his hand.

Again the coals moved. He looked wildly, anxiously, to see some new vision—but there was none.

In the grey light he sat alone with the Presence.

Then footsteps sounded far away, they dinned into his brain; he longed to rush out towards them, but the Presence held him back.

The slow ticking of a clock above his head seemed as the heavy tramp of men, the footsteps were coming nearer; in a dark corner he seemed to see rough men with kindly faces searching fields with lanterns.

A rolling of thunder sounded in the distance.

He felt the approach of the footsteps nearer, nearer; he shuddered at the Presence, he dreaded the unknown.

All his frame was shaking, his haggard eyes stared before him blankly.

Then voices, real voices, hushed and terrible, and a knock at his door.

He was paralyzed at first, he could not rise; his hand was trembling violently, and his pipe fell to the floor.

Another knock! He made a great effort and staggered towards the door.

There were the lanterns and three men in cloaks soaked with rain.

Still the wind prayed. He stood staring at his guests.

One of them began nervously to move his lips.

"Good God! man, speak—tell me, tell me—is she dead—is—she—DEAD?"

The three men started.

Their silence answered him. Thus he learned that the Presence was Death.

FAIRIES

WILL you come with me to Fairyland?
　　Come when evening shadows gently fall:
Just across yon bridge there is a wood
　　Where the fairies have a nightly ball.
Underneath the boughs they gaily trip,
　　Laughing little elves and nymphs and fays,
But they must not see us, for they dread
　　Mortal people and all mortal ways.

Here, beside the brooklet, let us lie,
　　Then I think the revels we shall see.
Hark! I hear them coming; I am sure
　　Nought but fairy laughter that can be.
Little partners have a deal to say,
　　Secrets to be told in anxious ears;
But they must not see us, or their hearts
　　Will be pit-a-pattering with fears.

Let us watch their dances all unseen,
　　See them laugh the moonlight into day,
When the wood is bathed with early dew,
　　And the fairies slowly trip away;
In our hearts we too may join the dance,
　　With the happy fairies we may move:
We are just as happy, you and I,
　　Living in the Fairyland of Love!

TAKE HEED, ALL YE LOVERS

To never cease praising one's lady to a pretty maiden
Is like unto asking a lily in a large garden:
" Are not all the other flowers fairer far than thou ? "

TO F. G. S. AND S. S. S.

THE ATHLETE AND THE ÆSTHETE

A BRAWNY athlete with an æsthete stood
  Trembling before the fast-closed gates of heaven.
One was relying on his " lovely soul,"
  The other on his play in an eleven.
One wore a velvet coat—ambrosial locks
  Peeped underneath his most " artistic " hat ;
The other wore white knickers, and he grasped
  Half-nervously a presentation bat.
Each gazed upon the other scornfully,
  Feeling that he alone would enter in ;
One thought that Art was idiotic rot,
  The other that to live for sport was sin.

Saint Peter kept them waiting many hours.
  At last, however, he produced the keys.
At the first jangle each man made a dash,
  But Peter cried out, " Gently, if you please."
He held them back : " And now I'd like to know
  What claims you make to pass within these gates."
Said one, " I have a very lovely soul ; "
  The other cried, " I bat and lift huge weights."

Saint Peter laughed in quite a nasty way,
   "Go forth," he said : " you cannot pass to-day.
There's no room for a bragging athlete here,
   Nor for a weak conceited popinjay.
Learn from each other for a year or twain
   In Purgatory, ere you come again.
There are two things we will not have up here :
   Brain without muscle, muscle without brain."

After long years the æsthete reappeared,
   Raising huge dumb-bells o'er his manly chest ;
Beside him was his dear athletic friend,
   Perusing Shakespeare with a wondrous zest.
Saint Peter met them with a smile most bland,
And introduced them to the happy band.
" A healthy body and a lovely mind,"
Said he, " are perfect only when combined."

Saint Peter first addressed them, you will note,
   As a policeman would.   The second time
As old Kháyyam.   This latest speech of his
   Suggests the language of a pantomime !

THE HIPPO MANIAC

THE poet had a fresh sorrow.

He could not find a passable word to rhyme with " hippopotamus " !

At first this was merely a slight worry. He did not trouble much about it, ate his meals as regularly as cash would allow, and smoked an occasional pipe.

Then it became a nuisance. It haunted him, and he found himself pondering over it during his meals; moreover, small hippopotami appeared in the wreaths of smoke.

Finally, it became a terror. His brain became as hot as Satan's kingdom; hippopotami haunted him night and day; he ceased meals, and substituted sponge-cakes at intervals.

He was a poet whose whole character might be summed up by saying that he preferred Swinburne to Wordsworth ! His personal appearance resembled a codfish with emotions.

When, as was his wont, he wore a clerical hat which looked like a grotesque black halo, he resembled a canonized codfish—a new patron for fishermen !

F

He dissected himself in print for the supposed delectation of his public.

On one occasion he had been detected quoting letters from recipients of presentation copies of his works as "opinions of the press."

Since when many people had firmly declined to believe that he was mad.

He occasionally varied poetry with begging letters written for those who deserved so much that they got nothing.

He suffered from the horrible disease "views about everything."

One was apt to forget that he was a man until one caught sight of his trousers—frayed trousers symbolic of frayed manhood.

He had had a somewhat similar trouble over another beast—the rhinoceros.

He wished to send a bitingly sarcastic rhyme to a gentleman bubbling over with common-sense—a practical gentleman, who was his pet aversion. What could be more biting or more sarcastic than to compare him to a rhinoceros? Yet to do so in rhyme was a Herculean task—oh, the pity o't!—nothing rhymed with "rhinoceros."

At last he got out of the difficulty by forwarding to his pet aversion the following weird metrical proverb :—

" *To ask a 'practical' man's opinion of a frail poem,*
  Is like unto setting a rose beneath the nostrils of a
    rhinoceros,
  And asking the beast, ' Hath it not a sweet scent ?' "

It was not poetry, but the poet thought it a great success.

His pet aversion's reply was something about "the effusion of a mass of nerves and nonsense," which might be considered smart by those who delight in alliteration.

A hippopotamus, however, seemed a worse beast to tackle than a rhinoceros.

The poet wrapped damp towels around his brow, but still the huge feet of a hippopotamus seemed to be cake-walking on his head.

He endeavoured to interest himself in *Please Bend Over*, a new schoolboy's weekly, but to no avail.

So, tearing the towels off, seizing a hat, he rushed into the streets of London with wild eyes, rough hair, shabby raiment, pursued by the mammoth hippos of his brain (he began to call them hippos for short!). As he emerged from his Brixton home he strongly resembled the mad hatter.

He proceeded at terrific speed. At the corner of the road was a stately edifice known as The Barrow and Spade. Through the open door sounded the slow sensuous music of a popular waltz.

A fellow-worshipper of the Muse begged of him to sip nectar with him in the form of a small Bass, but he rushed past, scarcely noticing, and crying, "What rhymes with 'hippopotamus'? My kingdom for a rhyme!"

The cry was repeated by several street Arabs, and became a Brixton catch-phrase during the week.

The fellow-worshipper returned to his pals, suggesting that " poor —— had got D.T.'s."

Some one else replied that he had only got " poet's licence."

The poet later on passed a flower-shop. A tall syren, with fluffy hair and saucer eyes, smiled at him.

She had been warned against him by her mother, who declared she could see he had " the poets' way with women" (who is not a psychologist nowadays?).

The daughter naturally, therefore, delighted in carrying on a violent flirtation.

It was the poet's wont to give her verses, or boxes of cigarettes, or chocolates; but to-day he stood dazed, asked her if she had any flower which rhymed with " hippopotamus;" " if not, fare thee well!" and rushed on.

Some grimy old women, standing on grimier doorsteps, and hugging yet grimier babies, laughed weirdly as he passed.

" My! Ain't 'e bloomin' off it?" murmured the syren to the small urchin who ran messages and cleaned out the shop.

" Oh, that ain't nothin', miss. Yer should see our dad under the booze!" was the reply.

From the flower-shop the poet trudged for many weary miles until there were holes in his boots and blisters on his feet.

Hippos still pursued him, large and small. He felt like the owner of a performing troupe, only he seemed owned rather than owner.

On one occasion he asked a waitress for a small hippopotamus instead of a small Läger.

For days he wandered on, sleeping by the roadside, by some merciful providence escaping the police.

On the fifth day, as he lay in a meadow, just beneath an advertisement of "Tarter's Little Tummy Pills," there came to him two nigger minstrels on their way to town.

Their picturesque garb and cheery faces were as a ray of dusky sunshine in his darkness.

He soon explained to them the sorrow of his life, and almost fainted with terror at the approach of a cow and a calf.

One of the minstrels commenced playing that touching ditty, "Where is my wandering boy to-night?" on his banjo. Then, after making most anxious and kindly inquiries as to his worldly wealth, and after ascertaining that this amounted to barely sixpence, they left him, suggesting that if nothing rhymed with "hippopotamus," something might rhyme with "hippo."

It really seemed a brilliant idea at first, but in time it lost its brilliance.

The next day the poet almost committed suicide in the public library of a town blessed by Mr. Carnegie.

He had been consulting a rhyming dictionary.

The librarian, a specimen of the wizened wisdom of a weary world (which sounds like a quotation from the classics, but isn't!), had gazed at him as the editor of *Mighty Thoughts* might gaze at a stray copy of *Comic Chirps*.

Later on in the day, the poet laid him down beside a brook, and began to cut his hair with a paper-knife —a difficult and rather painful process, as the knife was blunt and the hair thick.

He vaguely imagined that he resembled Moses in the bulrushes.

He was hiding from the ever-present hippos behind a friendly shrub, hoping that the loss of his hair would cool his brain.

While he was thus engaged an elderly lady passed by. On seeing him she started and screamed, but soon calmed down and handed him a tract from a bag at her side.

"Have a care, madam! have a care!" the poet murmured, gently drawing her beneath the shrub. "Do you not espy yon hippopotami? They come towards us! Lie here, and all will be well. I will protect you."

He pointed with a trembling finger at some distant sheep, the while he clasped her around the waist. "Sir, leave go! how dare you!" exclaimed the lady, in the usual formula of the British matron.

" But, madam—the hippopotami!"

Then she looked at him kindly. "Ah, yes," she whispered, "poor fellow! Will you wait here quietly while I fetch my brother?"

She left him ; but when presently he saw her in the distance with a tall parson and a stout individual carrying a rope, he bolted off like the tuppenny tube.

Finally he sank down utterly exhausted.

The hippos stood all around him, but he did not mind. They seemed less harmful than he thought they would be. He still murmured, "What rhymes with 'hippopotamus'?" but now he dreaded the creature with the rope more than all the beasts in the world.

Soon the trees, the grass, the hippos began to revolve, then everything became a misty white, and he knew no more.

* * * * *

He awoke in a cottage and in a state of stupefaction.

A motherly soul equally incapable of a past or a future was stroking his forehead, and at the foot of the bed on which he lay a small boy was riding a toy horse, a paper cap on his head, and a tin sword in his hand. The first thing which struck the poet was the strange absence of hippopotami—it seemed unnatural!

Then it dawned upon him. The small boy—a modern St. George—had slain them all.

Beckoning the boy to him, he asked him if this were not so.

The small boy put his tongue in his cheek, and gazed "from heaven to earth, from earth to heaven," but, after many secret signs from his mother, nodded his head.

With tears in his eyes the poet thanked him. "Brave laddie! brave laddie!" was all he could say, although he was not a bit Scotch, nor an actor!

Then he lay for some time thinking, until at last a great idea struck him—he would no more write poetry, but prose !

So, after sending for money from Brixton, and rewarding the cottagers (including St. George !), he returned home.

*   *   *   *   *

His first novel was a decided success, and so have been his other prose works—he is now one of the most popular writers of the day.

He retains a dim recollection of a strange wandering, of hippopotami, and a small boy on a toy horse, but what the Dickens it all means he can never make out.

A fellow-worshipper of the Muse and a flower-shop syren tell him about some mysterious evening, and once a scrubby street-boy yelled out after him, "What rhymes with 'hippopotamus'? My kingdom for a rhyme!" It is all very perplexing.

He never refers to this chapter of his life when interviewed in the weekly papers.

The fellow-worshipper, as he reads his friend's latest, while smoking a tuppenny cigar, says to himself that "genius and madness go together," and fingers gratefully ten gold-uns which he borrowed from a genius the day before !

A CHALLENGE ACCEPTED

AFTER the publication of the foregoing story I received, under the above heading, the following verses from a reader evidently sorry for the poet :—

" When our boat was upset by the great hippopotamus,
   'Twere absurd to contend that just then there was
      not a muss,*
For we all of us felt that he'd sent to the bottom us."

" Thy darts can subdue e'en a lovesick rhinoceros
   (That's a compliment surely—you needn't be cross,
      Eros)."

   Even with the aid of Shakespeare, however, I fear the writer has not found " a passable *word* " to rhyme with either beast !

   * *Muss*, a scramble.—*Antony and Cleopatra.*

INCONSISTENCIES

I MET a small fat man who loved to prate
Of " certainties " about our future state.
I asked him to give proofs of what he saith ;
He cried, " There are no proofs, we must have faith."

I knew a dreary man, both lean and sad,
Who vowed that all our modern plays are bad ;
I asked him if to plays he'd often been ?
He answered, " No, but *East Lynne* twice I've seen."

EVASION

HE played a " little, sad thing."
He wrote that " little, sad thing."
It was a very bad thing in a mournful minor key.
The girl he serenaded
Said (and thus the truth evaded),
" How men ever write such music is a miracle to
me !"

LONDON EFFUSIONS

I.—LOVE AND A VIOLIN

TRIM little maid, with your violin,
All unconcerned 'midst the city's din,
Tripping along with a radiant smile,
Thinking perchance of HIM the while !
May you and your happiness never part !
May you live in a heaven of Love and Art !

II.—THE ONE RIGHTEOUS MAN

ON Sundays you may see him as a rule
Near Marble Arch, upon a wooden stool,
The man who found the world as black as night,
And knows that he was born to set it right.
Yet things go on the same, one must confess,
Despite his strange conceit and wordiness !

III.—AN ENTREATY

IN Regent Street, dear country cousins all,
  Who come at times to see the town (and me !),
I prithee let me leave you for a while,
  And linger in some tavern peacefully,
There to enjoy a long, refreshing drink,
While you choose wondrous " things which will not
    shrink."

AN AMATEUR

"What rage for fame attends both great and small !
Better be d—d than mentioned not at all."
JOHN WOLCOT.

He's an actor, a wonderful actor
  (He's really an excellent fellow !),
He'll play "Shylock" or "Sherlock" or "Gentleman
    Joe"
  Or he'll "have a shot" at "Othello."

He's an author, a rising young author,
  His novels and plays are immense,
While his poems, though soulful, are chaste as a rose,
  "Are they published?" "Yes (at his expense !)."

He's ev'rything under the sun,
  His life is unceasingly gay,
He never feels slow ; it's rich fun, don'cher know,
  To *live* "in an amateur way !"

THE WANT

HE had chambers, which his aunts—ladies of fashion—when they saw, described as "luxurious;" which a middle-class cousin, not wholly unconnected with oil-cloth and a patent pill, had once described—with a faint suggestion of family pride—as "palatial;" and which his landlady often described as "the finest in the City"—especially if he showed an inclination to discuss the expense.

He stood smoking, his back to the fire—a *tableau vivant* of the British householder. His complexion, owing to everlasting cigarettes, was the colour of absinthe mixed with water.

Before him lounged some friends in armchairs, also smoking. Conversation never for an instant failed—yet he felt there was something wanting.

The next day a piano came.

His friends played selections from the latest musical comedy, Sousa, Wagner, and *St. Paul*—each according to his own temperament, some also sang of "Mrs. 'Enry 'Awkins," "The Village Smithy," and "Mélisande," while he himself began to learn his notes—yet there was something wanting.

The next day a parcel of the latest fiction came, and he found himself mildly interested in the volumes —yet still he was haunted by the want.

Then a new smoking mixture came with a new patent pipe; also a pianola came, accompanied by a gramophone—yet still the want remained.

So he took to writing a novel, even as some take to drink—to drown sorrow, and for one ever-memorable week (including Sunday) he put his soul on paper.

On the seventh day he destroyed what he had made in fury—then there seemed to be a greater want than ever.

The want got on his nerves. It was really very trying—moreover, it was becoming expensive.

A tonic came which looked like ink, and tasted like hairwash—yet after a fortnight's trial its effect was *nil*.

Finally a little girl came and talked with him, while her father discussed the fiscal question with an obliging friend who shone unnoticed at local Conservative meetings.

She was a very simple little girl with merry eyes and dark hair—wearing the prettiest of white frocks.

She taught him in a marvellously short space of time that he was rather a selfish, useless fool, and caused him to make a great many excellent resolutions for her sake—nearly all of which he kept!

He found the rummaging out and cultivation of his good points decidedly interesting.

She left her heart in the luxurious palatial chambers which were " the finest in the City," and (little knowing what she had done!) supplied the want.

ATONEMENT

A MONOLOGUE

SCENE—*A dusty, deserted room in Paris. The only furniture, a bench and a table. An old, torn curtain,* L.C., *divides off what has been a sleeping apartment.* C., *a window through which may be seen an illuminated church clock.* R.C., *a door.*

CARL ROIS *staggers in. Moonlight displays him. He is of haggard appearance, aged 28, dressed roughly, handsome.*

CARL ROIS (*in a dazed manner, creeping slowly towards the curtain*).

The little room where she was sleeping—my Babette! The door by which I entered—a year ago.

They tell me now the attic is haunted, no one will dare enter it, and no one saw the murder—no one but I! How dark and still it was when, mad with hatred, with jealousy, I stole in here to kill the girl I loved— to kill her just because she loved another man!

How I trembled as I crouched among the shadows to hide the shining knife!

I gazed upon her sleeping for a long while, and she looked like a fairy, so peaceful and happy, with her golden hair on the white pillow, that I almost cried aloud as I raised the knife, "O God! I can't do it! I can't do it!"

But my brain was on fire, a thousand devils whispered in my ears, "Strike! strike! Are you afraid at the last? Are you a coward? Strike!" So I shut fast my eyes and stabbed her. She gave no cry, and I rushed out into the night, flying from the man she loved.

Then escape! How I have wandered through the wide world! trembling at every sound, strange voices ever crying, "You are a murderer—a *murderer!* You may escape the man you have wronged, but you cannot escape yourself, Carl Rois! Your hands are bloody, and your life is accursed. You cannot escape yourself!"

Good God! it was not life, it was hell—a hell of torment and despair.

So this is the haunted room where the murder was —a year ago.

(*Brings forth from his coat a long knife which glitters in the moonlight, gazes at it and slowly feels the blade.*) It is a sharp blade (*with horror*). How brightly it gleams! brightly as that other blade—a year ago! (*He lays the knife on the floor, and with a groan falls sobbing on his knees.*)

Babette! my little Babette! I am coming to you. Perhaps, dear, after long years I may see you, when

the blood is washed from me. God is very merciful.
I have always loved you, Babette, always. Can you
and the man you loved forgive, he who now will never
have his revenge on earth? I have done much
penance, dear; have suffered long! I was mad—a
year ago. (*He lifts the knife, gazes at it half smiling,
then bends his head in prayer, quickly crosses himself,
and raises it.*) Gentle Christ! Holy Mother! Babette!
forgive! (*Plunges the knife into his breast.*) If I can
I—will—atone.

(*He falls near the curtain. Outside may be heard
the church clock striking twelve.*)

CURTAIN.

G

LOVE-SONG

SLEEP among the shadows,
 Sleep, my love,
While the stars are shining,
 Thy home above.
While all is silent, while all is still,
Sleep, where no living thing shall do thee ill.

Sleep, O my darling,
 Peacefully ;
May thy waking thoughts, dear,
 Be just of me !
Loving each other ever night and day,
We shall be very near though far away.

Sleep among the shadows,
 Sleep, my love,
While the tall trees whisper,
 Thy home above.
God in His mercy, queen of my heart,
Keep us from every sorrow while apart !

MOONLIGHT AND DAYLIGHT

I MADE a rhyme one dreamy moonlight night,
While gazing in thine eyes, my heart's delight;
I thought 'twould be remembered for all time,
It seemed to be so wonderful a rhyme.

Next day to my great joy it had not flown :
I seized a pen and quickly wrote it down.
Alas ! that rhyme away I had to fling,
The daylight made it seem a paltry thing !

AT A DANCE

REFLECTIONS OF AN OLD STAGER

THE happy partners glide in dreamy joy,
    To music slow,
And flashing eyes, like little lamps of love,
    Flit to and fro.

While merry laughter echoes through the room,
    See! here and there,
A modern gallant leads across the floor
    His lady fair.

So once, in days, alas! how long ago!
    I danced with you,
And in a secret nook love's old, old tale
    Was told anew!

TWO FANCIES

I.—OUR LADY'S FLOWERS

A GREAT actor died, and many crowded to his funeral.

Most came full of sorrow, for they had known and loved him in his lifetime, or remembered times when he had stirred their souls; some came from curiosity; others from a sense of duty.

His grave was covered with flowers sent by many famous folk.

At night, when the huge gates of the cemetery were fast closed, and all was very still, an angel came from heaven to take some flowers to Our Lady from his grave.

Every day angels bring Our Lady, from the graves on earth, the flowers which have been given by the warmest hearts.

As the angel stood over the actor's grave, she groped among the flowers until she found a bunch of violets. An envelope was tied to it, on which was written, " With love and gratitude."

The angel laid the violets before Our Lady's throne.

*   *   *   *   *

In a dingy lodging a little actress dreamed that night that Our Lady smiled on her, and that in her garment were the violets which she had placed upon the actor's grave—a poor little thank-offering for all his goodness to her in bad times, yet given with all her heart.

She visited the grave the next day, and lo! the violets were gone.

*   *   *   *   *

Perhaps, when she and the actor meet in heaven, Our Lady will make her understand!

II.—THE MOST BEAUTIFUL THING ON EARTH

A MAN once was seeking for the most beautiful thing on earth.

Many seek for it, but he differed from others, for it had been told him that, when he found it, a white rose should suddenly appear in his button-hole—that was to be the sign.

He travelled in many lands, saw the great sights of the world, yet found it not after many years of searching.

At last an angel came to him as he sat listening to a famous opera, and told him she was sent to show it him, for he had been seeking long enough.

They went from the crowded building together, and

the angel led him through brilliantly lighted thorough-fares and many dark sad streets, until they reached a small mean-looking house.

They passed upstairs, and the angel left him, whis-pering that, although he could see all, he would be unseen.

The room was poorly furnished, but everything was spotlessly clean.

On a bed lay a young mother, looking weary, but very happy.

By her side sat a wise-looking old body, crooning a lullaby while she nursed a baby-boy. Opposite the bed hung a bracket, on which was an image of the Holy Mother and her Child, with lighted candles and some flowers.

The man saw that they were all white roses.

The mother was smiling dimly and calling for her child.

When she held him in her arms, she spoke in a trembling, silvery voice. Then she kissed him, and spoke no more for joy.

Death had kissed her and passed on, leaving her with Life and Love.

The man was stealing from the room, when he noticed a white rose in his button-hole.

Unseen, he placed it in the outstretched fingers of the baby.

As he journeyed home he knew that there is nothing on earth more beautiful than the birth of a little child.

VENUS AND TANNHÄUSER

SUGGESTED BY WAGNER'S OPERA, ACT I.
SCENE 1

FAIR is the Venusberg, a realm of peace,
Filled with the holy fragrance of fresh flowers,
Echoing ever with the songs of birds,
With plaintive sleep-songs, peaceful lullabies,
Sung by the nymphs who dwell in Fancyland.
Bright is the Venusberg, there comely forms
Flit to and fro, while rippling laughter sounds,
And with the evening hours the shadows creep
Like spectres moving in some weird, wild dance,
Beneath the mystic radiance of the moon.
Calm is the Venusberg, the stately swans
Glide slowly down the lake as sometimes men
Glide sadly down the silent lake of Time.
Within this land no mortal ever trod
Save one, Tannhäuser, knight of war and song,
Skilled in the fight and minstrel of renown.
It chanced once on a time as Venus sat
Holding her court, surrounded by her train
Of courtiers, from the toilful land of men
There came to her this weary wanderer
In blood-stained armour, holding with both hands

His aching, dizzy brow the while he reeled,
And almost fell from weariness of foot.
Seeking a refuge from the griefs of earth,
Worn out and buffeted by years of strife,
Tannhäuser came to her, his spirit full
Of wistful longing for some realm of peace.
Around him ran the nymphs with wondering looks,
And shyly touched his armour each in turn,
While Venus gently stroked his long dark hair,
Soothed his sad soul with many words of love.
Then the great warrior, as a little child,
Lay down at Beauty's feet in ecstasy.
Amid the roses and the singing-birds,
Of no account was held the flight of time;
Till all his sadness slowly passed away,
His heart grew strong again, once more he felt
A strong, brave man, and cried out for release :
" Fair Venus, Queen of Beauty and these realms,
Thou solace of my sorrow, ne'er can I
Forget thee who hast saved me from despair.
It was so sweet to gaze and gaze on thee,
To feel thy kisses showered on me alone,
To know no trouble, but to dream in peace.
Glad in the glorious ecstasy of love.
Thus, were I not of mortal birth, I trow
I would be glad to ever dwell with thee,
Yet now I long for life with all its joys,
With all the grim array of mortal woes.
I yearn for bitter trials overcome,
I pray for conflicts, sigh for victories.

Ah! let me go where, as of yore, I may
Live in the mortals' land, apart from thee.
This Venusberg, as some enchanting dream,
Grows empty to the sleeper who awakes.
For me its joys are empty now: I feel
The dull monotony of endless rest,
The weary luxury of selfish sloth."
He ceased.   A solemn stillness seemed to fall
On all around.   Then Venus rose and begged,
While from her eyes great tears rolled slowly down
Upon her heaving breast, that he would stay
For ever in her realm of dreams and love:
" Ah! cruel heart, thou boastest mortal blood.
Is it, then, like a man to seize the joys,
To wring all sweetness from the fruit of life
Only to sate the evil lust of greed?
When thou hast tasted fully of my love,
To go forgetful of the broken heart
Here left behind, if gaining great renown
In lands afar by deeds of mighty worth,
Yet here renowned but as a cruel curse
Which came upon us in an evil hour?
If this be manliness, in truth it is
A gift one should not seek for from the Gods!
Long have I soothed thy sorrows, sung thee songs
Until thy weary head was lulled to sleep,
Given thee all my soul's fond gift of love
For this reward—thy love in turn for me.
When suddenly thy heartless, cruel words,
Like some keen daggers plunged within my breast,

Render me dizzy, ah! I had not dreamed
A son of woman e'er could be so harsh,
Yet, though I blame thee, is my love unchanged.
Stay with us, O my king, I thee implore,
And I will sing thee all the songs thou lov'st;
And when thou tirest of my songs the nymphs
Shall dance for thee, or I will gather flowers
And crown thy brow with garlands I have made.
Thus will we live each day, and when the night
Steals o'er us every little dreaming star
Shall smile upon us, envying our joy.
Stay! for without thee life will be as death."
Tannhäuser stood before her in the sun,
With head bent low, while in his hand he clasped
His gleaming silver sword as if to hold
Thoughts of his manhood ever in his heart.
Then Venus with a moan raised high her arms,
Falling in supplication at his feet.
Her hair was all in golden disarray,
Yet still he stood and heeded not her woe,
Then with stern face, all pity crushed and killed,
He calmly cast aside the weeping Queen:
"Go, traitor-heart!" she cried. "Go from my sight!"
Then, "No, ah! no; he cannot leave me thus.
Go with no cursing from the lips of her
Whose love thou hast first won, then trampled on."
So silently he started on his way,
Journeying onward to the land of men,
Yet all the while there sounded in his ears
That sad, low moaning in the Venusberg.

A "MIGHT-HAVE-BEEN"

"Of all sad words of tongue or pen,
  The saddest are these : ' It might have been.' "
                                    J. G. WHITTIER.

"Hopes are like predictions ; for every one that is realized there are a thousand which do not come to pass."—ETIENNE COENILHE (1721).

HE is a fine-looking old English gentleman with silvery hair and a voice full of music.

He invariably visits the club about five o'clock, partakes of a whisky-and-soda, and buries himself in a daily paper or one of the learnèd reviews ; but often I have seen pretty little editions of the poets peeping out of his coat-pockets, and once I espied him reading Keats' *The Eve of St. Agnes !*

His face suggests half-soldier, half-poet. At about eight o'clock he usually returns to the club, and is ever ready for a conversation.

It was about a year ago that he first spoke to me. He had always interested me very much, but, as a mere youngster, I had, of course, never addressed him. By the mysterious law of affinity—I learned from him afterwards—I also had interested him.

On the evening he spoke first to me we were alone together in the smoking-room, save for the presence of the invariable club nuisance—a fat gentleman, who made a large collection of all the most interesting papers, sat on them, and went to sleep!

I happened to have with me that night a new and very beautiful edition of Shelley's Poems, which had been sent me for review; and I think it was the sight of this which decided him to make my acquaintance.

At any rate, he turned over the leaves of the volume with all the ardour of the book-lover, and we entered upon a lively discussion on some of the footnotes, which were a special feature of the edition.

The discussion, indeed, became so lively that the club nuisance awoke with a start, yawned, and left us to ourselves.

From Shelley we passed on to many other subjects, and we soon felt that the strong bond of friendship was between us—a bond which can never be affected by either age or sex.

It was late in the evening some weeks afterwards that he told me his story, as I sat in his chambers.

He spoke very slowly as he smoked, and in the light of the fire (for we had been talking in the fire-light) his face seemed to me more wonderful than ever.

"There is a day-dream very dear to me," he began. "It is sad, but I would be very sorry to part with it, for it brings me much comfort in a rather lonely old age. I fear sometimes lest it may perish, lest stern reality may destroy happy fancy, and I may lose the power to call it up before me at my will.

"Then I take from its rack this old pipe, lean back in this armchair—one of the dearest of my friends—and, as I smoke, gaze upon this picture.

"In the midst of lovely country is a little house. It stands all alone, very, very old—some say five hundred years—and around it seem ever to trip gallants and dames of olden time in a stately phantom minuet.

"A quaint sundial is on the lawn, and beside it stand two figures—a girl and a boy. Around them are summer flowers. It is a pretty picture, very full of joy—and it moves!

"Presently the girl and boy go within the house, smiling and talking, arm-in-arm; then, just as they are disappearing, they kiss.

"They are on their honeymoon—a pair of married lovers, desiring nothing save to be alone together.

"Then the picture vanishes. My pipe, as a rule, is smoked out, and sometimes, rising, I draw aside the curtains and look out upon the night.

"London's brilliantly lighted streets are below; I hear the muffled sound of traffic, and above shine many stars.

"I draw back the curtains, return to this old chair, and think long and sadly—sometimes not without a few tears.

"For I am the boy of the picture. But it is only a day-dream of what might have been—of what might have been had not the girl's death prevented it long years ago, and ordained that my heart's desire should be fulfilled only in an old man's dreams.

"I sent her flowers—roses of wonderful tints, and great lilies; but I did not attend her funeral. My love was too great for that. Why should we hasten to gather around the bodies of our dead?

"It is their souls, not their bodies, we have known and loved.

"And when those sad, pale corpses, so full of terror —which none of us can really wish to see—are laid beneath the earth, it is memory of them alive, not dead, which will give us sometimes comfort, sometimes strength—a certain immortality!

"'To pay respect to the dead.' How grotesquely formal is the phrase!

"How I detest the black bands and trousers and ties, and the *crêpe* and the memorial cards, and all the hideous paraphernalia of manufactured grief!

"Far better that our dead should pass gently out of our lives like happy dreams, than that we should have such gruesome recollections of their endings as that!

"It seems to be the fashion nowadays among many people to laugh at or despise love, but that is only because they have never really known what love is. Some day, I hope, if I can, to go and live alone in the little house, and you must come and see me there sometimes, if you will—yes! and I hope, some day, you will bring a wife with you, and you must let me give you both my blessing!"

THE SILVER LINING

THE point of this little tale is that artists are, as Mr. Chesterton wrote of Charles Dickens, easy to hurt, but impossible to kill.

Thisbe and other Verses burst upon the world rather, I fear, like a damp squib.

In one instance, the work written by one who lived on Grape Nuts in order that he might buy Homer, was reviewed by a literary rhinoceros!

"This book of poems seems to us full of soulful silliness."

Thus wrote Monsieur le reporter, mildly attempting alliteration!

But among the notices of his book the author of *Thisbe and other Verses* inserted—

"'POEMS'—*The Vapid Review*."

THE END

CPSIA information can be obtained
at www.ICGtesting.com
Printed in the USA
LVHW100800180321
681833LV00015B/287

9 781293 041178